Autonomous As Breath

Secret Of Happiness And Success

@ Students & Parents

Rao Chalasani

Rao Chalasani

ISBN: 978-0-9979812-5-4

Published by

Creative Harmony

Fort Myers, Florida 33913

Table Of Contents

Chapters

Foreword

The collective wisdom of human spirit, built on innate strengths of individuals driven by insatiable desire for freedom and love of self and the rest, is the building block to preserve the gains made since organized living evolved unevenly throughout the world with agriculture maturing into industry and technology. The journey was never linear and fit the known expression of two steps forward and one step back. Progress was never in doubt even in the darkest periods because the Sun never let down the collective ambition. Life goes on only to witness a better future driven by the intangible assets of freedom and love of self and the rest.

The desire of the author is to translate the aforesaid intangible assets into an autonomous mode of behavior for a critical mass of individuals that can reverberate in the connected world now that has no precedence. Creativity and curiosity since birth in everyone can translate to happiness and success if a certain path is followed. The author methodically lists the steps that can be followed in daily life. It is unequivocally ambitious but very much within the realm of making it as autonomous as breath.

The author, Rao Chalasani, sincerely thanks Manoj Sam for being a supporter and available at every step to make unvarnished comments and thoughts to bring the book to completion.

1.

Curious Arun

Arun and Grandpa strolled into the park, the summer sun casting a warm glow over the lush greenery. They settled onto a weathered wooden bench, savoring every lick of their chocolate ice cream cones. Arun's eyes sparkled with curiosity as he turned to his grandfather.

Arun: “Pops, why are people nice sometimes and mean at other times?”

Grandpa smiled gently, his eyes crinkling at the corners. “Arun, people being nice is common because it’s part of human nature. But being mean sometimes is also human.”

Arun furrowed his brow, a hint of frustration in his voice. “Make it simple, Pops. Don’t confuse me.”

Grandpa nodded, sensing Arun’s earnest desire to understand. “Okay. Human beings are conflicted. They can show different feelings for the same thing at different times. Sometimes even small things can upset them.”

Arun looked down at his cone, deep in thought. “Why is that?”

Grandpa paused, choosing his words with care. “When a person is happy, smiles and nice words come naturally. But when they’re unhappy, those smiles disappear, and the opposite comes out. Your question is simple, but the answer is complex. If you understand why, you have the key to lifelong happiness. Happiness is a choice. It’s not as difficult to be happy as people think.”

Arun's eyes widened with intrigue. “Tell me more about it, please.”

Grandpa's gaze softened as he remembered. "Arun, I was overjoyed to hold you when you were just a few days old. When you cried, it was easy to sense that you needed something—hunger or discomfort. Your parents could understand your needs by the sound of your cries, even when others couldn't. Over the weeks and months, you began to understand what your parents meant by their expressions, and you responded with innocent smiles. A baby's smile is pure, beyond judgment, an expression of love, trust, and satisfaction."

Arun grinned. "That was ten years ago, Pops."

Grandpa chuckled, a nostalgic glint in his eye. "Yes, Arun. The bond between parents and their child from day one is crucial. A child learns every day, but the pace is different for each one."

As they finished their ice cream, Grandpa wrapped an arm around Arun's shoulders. The sun dipped lower, casting long shadows, but the warmth of their conversation lingered, a beacon of understanding in the twilight.

2.

The Golden Rules

Arun and Grandpa walk to their favorite park bench, the evening sun casting a golden glow around them. Grandpa's voice carried a warmth and wisdom that made Arun lean in closer, eager to absorb every word.

Grandpa: "Arun, there are eight Golden Rules.

They begin with a child's creativity and curiosity and culminate in happiness and success. The rules in between guide us on how to achieve that."

Arun's eyes sparkled with anticipation. "I can't wait to learn the Golden Rules."

Grandpa smiled, his voice steady and comforting. "The first rule is that curiosity and creativity are two sides of the same coin. Creativity won't flourish without curiosity, and it can't be sustained without it. This leads us to Rule 2: every child has both curiosity and creativity inherently, as part of their discovery process when they start observing the world around them.

"Rule 3 is about our DNA, which carries genetic information unique to each child. This identity suggests a hidden talent within each person, influenced partly by DNA and partly by environment, nutrition, and other factors."

Arun nodded, absorbing the information. "So, these rules are about recognizing what we already have?"

Grandpa's eyes twinkled with pride. "Exactly. Rules 2, 3, and 4 are observations. Rule 4 is the age-old saying, 'Prevention is better than cure.' Why suffer consequences if you can prevent them? Recognizing these rules sets the foundation. The real action comes with Rules 5 through 7, which help us actively pursue happiness and success."

Golden Rules

1. Curiosity and Creativity are two sides of the same coin.
2. Every child has both for keeps.
3. Everyone has a unique id with unique talent.
4. Prevention is better than cure.

Acronym: S O D — Autonomous as breath

S 5. Compete with self to succeed.
O 6. Be open to possibilities.
D 7. Manage choice and detach from chance.

8. Happiness and Success are realizable choices in reach.

Arun's face lit up with curiosity. "Tell me more, Grandpa. How do I practice these rules?"

Grandpa's expression grew serious yet encouraging. "Rule 5 is to compete with yourself to succeed. True competition means getting better than you were yesterday. It's more important to measure your own progress than to outsmart others. Competing with yourself reduces anxiety, anger, and hate. It's about self-improvement. When you do better than others, your relative score improves, but without unnecessary stress."

Arun's eyes widened in realization. "So, I don't have to worry about beating my friends. I can focus on improving myself."

Grandpa nodded, pleased with Arun's understanding. "Exactly. Now, Rule 6 is to be open to all possibilities. To find the best opportunities, you must be open-minded. Mahatma Gandhi is a great example. His strategies for freedom were different in South Africa and India, yet fundamentally compatible with the principles of human dignity and freedom. Being open to different possibilities allowed him to adapt and succeed."

Arun nodded eagerly. "That makes perfect sense, Pops. What about Rule 7?"

Grandpa's tone grew thoughtful. "Rule 7 is practical and profound. Things happen either by choice or by chance. You control your choices, but not the outcomes. Accepting outcomes as they are prevents unnecessary agony. This rule teaches the art of handling uncertainty.

"To clarify, Rule 7 has four components: a) make personal and voluntary choices aligned with societal interests, b) accept the outcomes as they come, c) never give up on ambitions that are good for you and society, and d) repeat this cycle of choice and detachment. Abraham Lincoln, for example, faced defeat seven times before becoming President of the United States. He accepted each defeat but never gave up his ambition, believing in himself and his cause."

Arun's face reflected understanding and determination. "I get it. Acceptance is a friend, not an enemy."

Grandpa beamed with pride. "Exactly, Arun. Remembering the actionable rules from 5 to 7 is easier with the acronym SOD: 'S' for competing with self, 'O' for openness, and 'D' for detachment."

As the sun began to set, casting long shadows over the park, Arun felt a deep sense of clarity and purpose. Grandpa's words had not only answered his questions but had also provided him with a roadmap for a fulfilling life.

Key Points of The Golden Rules

Overview:

- Eight Golden Rules guide a child's creativity and curiosity towards happiness and success.
- The rules include foundational observations and actionable steps for personal growth.

Golden Rules:

1.Curiosity and Creativity:

- Curiosity and creativity are intertwined.
- Creativity depends on sustaining curiosity.

2.Inherent Traits:

- Every child inherently possesses curiosity and creativity.
- These traits are essential for the discovery process.

3.DNA and Unique Talent:

- DNA carries unique genetic information for each child.
- This identity suggests a hidden talent, influenced by DNA, environment, nutrition, and other factors.

Prevention:

- The saying "Prevention is better than cure" emphasizes avoiding undesirable consequences when possible.

Actionable Rules:

1. Compete with Yourself:

- Focus on self-improvement rather than outsmarting others.

- Competing with self reduces anxiety, anger, and hate.
- Self-competition leads to better performance without unnecessary stress.

2. **Openness to Possibilities:**

- Be open-minded to find the best opportunities.
- Example: Mahatma Gandhi's adaptable strategies for freedom in different contexts.
- Openness allows for adapting and succeeding in various situations.

3. **Handling Uncertainty:**

- Things happen by choice or chance.
- Control your choices but accept outcomes as they come.

Four components:

a) Make personal choices aligned with societal interests.
b) Accept outcomes without unnecessary agony.

c) Maintain ambition that benefits self and society.
d) Repeat the cycle of choice and detachment.

Example: Abraham Lincoln's persistence despite multiple defeats.

Acronym for Actionable Rules:

SOD:

- S- for competing with self.
- O- for openness.
- D- for detachment.

Conclusion:

- Embracing these Golden Rules provides a roadmap for a fulfilling life.
- Acceptance and self-improvement are key to lifelong happiness and success.

3.

DAP

Arun and Grandpa played baseball in the morning until grandpa got tired. Arun teased grandpa and playfully asked for the next lesson.

Grandpa: "Arun, let me introduce you to DAP, a three-phase process to fulfill the promise of the Golden Rules."

Arun's excitement bubbled over. "Can't wait, Pops!"

Grandpa's voice was filled with warmth and wisdom. "Alright, Arun. The first phase is Discovery. This phase is for children aged three to nine. It's a time when curiosity and creativity blossom, laying the foundation for future learning."

Arun nodded, imagining himself as a little explorer. "What comes next?"

Grandpa continued, his tone steady and encouraging. "The second phase is Application, for those aged ten to twenty-five. This is when you take what you've discovered and start applying it to real-world situations, turning knowledge into action."

Arun's eyes sparkled with understanding. "So, this is where I am now, right?"

Grandpa smiled, "Exactly, Arun. The third phase is Purpose, for those over twenty-five. It's about finding and living your purpose, using your experiences and knowledge to contribute meaningfully to society."

Arun leaned in closer, hanging on to every word. “How do these phases connect?”

Grandpa’s expression grew thoughtful. “The age gradation is based on experience and varies from child to child. Graduates with distinction in the Discovery and Application phases can greatly shorten the time needed to find their Purpose. It’s not uncommon to complete the Application and Purpose phases by age 25. These phases are intricately linked to the development of the brain, mind, and creative spirit.”

As Grandpa spoke, Arun felt a sense of clarity and excitement about his own journey. The three phases—Discovery, Application, and Purpose—were not just steps but a meaningful path to becoming the best version of himself.

Grandpa’s words hung in the air, rich with emotion and wisdom, guiding Arun towards a future filled with promise and fulfillment.

Key Points: DAP

(Discovery, Application, Purpose)

Phase 1: Discovery

- Age Range: 3 to 9 years old.
- Focus: Curiosity and creativity blossom, laying the foundation for future learning.
- Goal: Encourage exploration and foundational understanding.

Phase 2: Application

- Age Range: 10 to 25 years old.
- Focus: Applying discovery in Phase 1 to real-world situations using mind as the tool.
- Goal: Gain knowledge in action and acquire practical skills.
- Current Status: Arun is in this phase.

Phase 3: Purpose

- Age Range: Over 25 years old.
- Focus: Finding and living one's purpose, using experiences and knowledge to contribute meaningfully to society.
- Goal: Achieve personal fulfillment and contribute to the community.

Connection Between Phases:

- **Experience-Based:** The phases are based on experience and can vary from child to child.
- **Potential for Acceleration:** Graduates with distinction in Discovery and Application can shorten the time needed to find their Purpose.
- **Interlinked Development:** Phases are linked to the development of the brain, mind, and creative spirit.

Overall Insight:

- The DAP process guides individuals towards becoming the best version of themselves.
- Each phase builds on the previous one, leading to a meaningful and fulfilling life.

Emotional Connection:

- Arun feels clarity and excitement about his journey through the phases.
- Grandpa’s wisdom and guidance are crucial in helping Arun understand and navigate these phases.

4.

Discovery

Arun and Grandpa sat on the porch, the evening sun casting long shadows. Arun's curiosity was palpable, his eyes wide with anticipation.

Arun: "I'm already in the second phase without even knowing how I did in the first phase."

Grandpa chuckled warmly. “Alright, let’s start from the beginning. For a child at the age of three, the brain isn’t developed enough to understand information logically. It makes sense to give practical input that’s easy to absorb and follow. At this age, the child knows the mother more than anyone else, followed by the father. As the child enters the fourth or fifth year of life, a teacher comes into their life. The absorption of what is said by these figures—let’s call it input; it is so natural that it’s easy for the child to accept, internalize, and make it a discipline.”

Arun: “You said that the input from parents and teachers would be easy to accept because it’s familiar to the child. I don’t quite understand that.”

Grandpa’s eyes softened. “Arun, a newborn exhibits three qualities early on: gratitude, love, and truth. Keen observation is needed to sense these qualities. When a child starts recognizing faces, the happiness and reaction to the mother’s face become evident in the child’s expressions. When their needs are attended to by the mother, the expression is one of gratitude. The child’s smile and movements when it sees the mother or father are expressions of deep love. The child can't hide its true feelings; it has no filters or inhibitions. These intrinsic qualities—gratitude, love, and truth—are the foundation of the first phase."

Arun frowned slightly. "I asked about the input from parents and teachers, and you're telling me about qualities. You're making it complicated."

Grandpa laughed gently. "Alright, who do you think you recognized first as a child?"

Arun: "My mom and dad."

Grandpa: "Who responded first when you cried?"

Arun: "My mom and dad."

Grandpa: "Who satisfied your hunger, cleaned you, and gave you a bath?"

Arun: "My mom and dad."

Grandpa: "Who responded to your smile just as quickly as they did to your cry?"

Arun: "My mom and dad. This is getting boring. What's the point?"

Grandpa's eyes twinkled with understanding. "Now you get the point. You're getting bored of my short questions, but your mom and dad never got bored responding to every cry, every smile, and every discomfort you had. You put 'mom' ahead of 'dad' because your mom carried you for nine months before your father saw you and treated you like a bundle of joy ever since."

Arun's face lit up with comprehension. "Now I understand. The same applies to the teacher, who comes after the parents to share knowledge and skills."

Grandpa smiled proudly. "Exactly. You also have other family members, neighbors, and the environment around you to influence your thinking. But a child under ten years lacks a developed mind to observe and think coherently to guide themselves. That's why parents, teachers, peer groups, and faith-driven institutions play a big role in shaping the child's character and behavior. Once you accept your parents and teachers as mentors, you internalize that belief, which acts like unforced faith, translating into behavior that represents gratitude, love, and truth. It becomes your first life-dictating discipline."

Arun: "Pops, you're like a teacher. I'm ready to learn more about these three values—gratitude, love, and truth."

Grandpa beamed. "I'm glad you called them values because that's what they are. They're unforced discipline, and you gradually own them. They reflect in your behavior throughout life. Gratitude is the highest value one can think of. A child develops gratitude naturally for what the parents do unconditionally. Love accompanies gratitude but needs more to sustain. 'Love thy neighbor' and 'radiate boundless love toward the entire world' mean that love has no boundaries."

Arun: "I also love Jackie."

Grandpa chuckled. "Dogs are a great example of gratitude, love, and truth. They don't run away when disciplined; they don't get angry and bite. Their love and gratitude for their owner are ever-present and true. No wonder children love dogs; they sense the same tenderness and purity in a dog's behavior."

Arun: "How about parental discipline?"

Grandpa's tone grew serious yet gentle. "Children are naturally mischievous. For example, a child opens a biscuit jar, believing no one is around, not knowing that Mom is watching. Mom has two choices. She can discipline the child sternly or run after the child with a playful smile, hug them, and explain the rules and consequences. It's tough love, but it's love that gets the message across."

Arun: "I know my mom would choose the second."

Grandpa: "Yes, she would. If discipline comes in the form of spanking, the child might lie to avoid it. A good parent provides an opportunity for the child to tell the truth. Once a child gets used to gratitude and love, truth becomes a habit, regardless of consequences. A friend once told me he never lies because it's a burden. If he lies, he must remember it to cover it up later. If he doesn't lie, he doesn't carry that burden. Elders should tell children not to lie, not just because it's immoral, but because it's for their own good."

Arun: "Wonderful, Pops."

Grandpa's eyes sparkled with pride. "Learning

these values early on means a lot for later life. Since they're unforced, it's easier for the child to accept and own them. As a result, many resistances and uncertainties disappear."

Arun: "You said curiosity and creativity are two sides of the same coin and that every newborn has them. Parents can make it easier for the child by following a path. You insist that everything goes well if the child practices three high values: gratitude, love, and truth."

Grandpa: "Yes, Arun, you've grasped it. Both you and your parents were in tune with this concept as you were growing. Thanks to them, you've successfully combined the discipline of these three values with the three actionable Golden Rules intuitively. Observe how well they fit together, lessening the burden of relying on memory."

Arun: "Please explain how my parents and I combined the three values with Golden Rules 5-7."

Grandpa: "Certainly. Golden Rule 5 states 'compete with yourself to succeed.' When you compete with yourself, the desire to understand and own the content is greater. Your parents never questioned your grades but helped you with additional tools like examples and stories. They told stories or read to you every night, helping you relate good values to good behavior. Your gratitude, love, and truthfulness deepened with their involvement. Competing with yourself would have been harder without proactive parents and teachers."

Arun: "Yes, I understand. Now, explain the combination with Golden Rule 6."

Grandpa: "Your parents helped you attend to your needs but never insisted on one way of doing things unless you were violating gratitude, love, and truth. This satisfies Golden Rule 6, which states 'Be open to possibilities.' They broadened your interests and provided confidence. I remember your preference for basketball over football, which your parents initially disagreed with due to your height. However, they saw your confidence and accepted your choice even before you demonstrated your moves. This openness to possibilities helped you grow."

Arun: "I see. Let's move on to Golden Rule 7."

Grandpa: "'Manage choice and detach from chance' is Golden Rule 7. It's easy to say but difficult to practice. The outcome isn't in your hands. The desire for an expected outcome motivates action. It takes courage to initiate action unattached to the outcome, but this has a powerful underpinning. Strong faith in the world's operation to reward hard work when aligned with individual and societal interests helps with detachment. This realization benefits practitioners of Golden Rule 7 throughout life. Remember when you made a bouquet for your mom's birthday and pricked your finger? You didn't give up despite the pain. You accepted the outcome as an interruption but continued to achieve your goal. This applies to both small tasks and life-altering decisions. You accept the outcome but don't give up if it's the right path and you have the option to start over. Earlier, I gave the example of President Abraham Lincoln."

Arun: "Thanks. It's nice of you to explain the three important Golden Rules in detail.

Pops, you are using both discovery and discipline

to explain Phase 1. Which one is correct?"

Grandpa: "You caught me. Discovery is correct, but in action, it's discipline. Parents discover that gratitude, love, and truth are inborn values. For the child, these values are instilled and taken as discipline. Recognition of these values as discipline is Discovery for the child. It's hard to see the same in two different ways, but it's a hidden fact."

Arun: "Okay, it satisfies my curiosity but is a bit confusing. Now that I'm in Phase 2, I can't wait to know how I did in Phase 1."

Grandpa smiled warmly. "In my judgment, you graduated from the first phase with distinction as you entered the second phase."

Arun's face lit up with joy. "Great, I'm very happy! Pops, at school, they say I'm always smiling and living in a different world. I feel like taking a vase with flowers to school. My mom and I spend a lot of time gardening, and we have fresh flowers all the time. Every school day, I can take fresh flowers and freshen up the vase on the teacher's table. What do you think? Will they call me crazy?"

Grandpa's eyes light up with pride. "Arun, that's a

wonderful idea. Your friends will understand why you're always smiling. They might call you crazy if you start laughing for no reason, but your smile lights up others. It's a great feeling to have. Don't be surprised if a few others follow your example. Your teachers will be happy too."

Arun: "Thanks, Pops."

Key Points: Discovery Phase

Brain Development and Input:

- Children aged three to nine are in the Discovery phase.
- At this age, the brain is not fully developed for logical understanding.
- Practical input, especially from parents and teachers, is crucial and easy for children to absorb.

Role of Parents and Teachers:

- Parents, followed by teachers, are the primary influences on a child's development in this phase.
- Parents and teachers' input is familiar and easily accepted by the child.
- They play a crucial role in shaping the child's character and behavior.

Intrinsic Qualities of a Child:

- Gratitude, love, and truth are intrinsic qualities of a child.
- These qualities are observed through the child's reactions to caregivers and surroundings.

Discipline and Learning:

- Discipline in this phase is about instilling these values through natural, unforced interactions.
- Gratitude, love, and truth become the child's first life-dictating discipline.

- Parental Role in Discipline:
- Parents discipline with love and understanding, guiding the child's behavior without harshness.
- Truthfulness is encouraged through providing opportunities for the child to tell the truth.

Combining Values with Golden Rules:

- The combination of gratitude, love, and truth with Golden Rules 5-7 is crucial for holistic development.
- These values help in understanding and applying the Golden Rules effectively.

Openness to Possibilities:

- Parents encourage openness to possibilities, allowing the child to explore and make choices within the framework of gratitude, love, and truth.

Acceptance and Resilience:

- Children learn acceptance and resilience through experiences like making mistakes and trying again.

Detachment:

- Golden Rule 7, "Manage choice and detach from chance," teaches the child to accept outcomes and not be discouraged by setbacks.
- Emotional Growth: The Discovery phase is not just about learning but also emotional growth and understanding.

Personal Development:

- The phase lays the foundation for personal development and sets the tone for future phases.

Child's Perception:

- Arun's perception of his childhood experiences and learnings reflects the essence of the Discovery phase.

Conclusion:

The Discovery phase is about laying a strong foundation of values and behavior that shape a child's future.

5.

Application

Arun looked at his grandfather with a mix of excitement and apprehension. "Pops, I'm ready for Phase 2."

Grandpa smiled warmly, his eyes reflecting pride and tenderness. "You're almost eleven now, ready to explore the depths of your mind. Phase 1 laid the groundwork, disciplining your brain. In Phase 2, it's about engaging your questioning mind, applying what you've learned to delve deeper. You'll discover so much more as you gain knowledge."

"But Pops," Arun interrupted, brows furrowed in curiosity, "aren't the mind and brain the same?"

Grandpa: “The distinction between mind and brain is not straightforward. You know where the brain is and how it functions. The mind has no physical space. Since it influences the brain, most assume it is in the brain. Without getting into expert opinions, let us settle on mind and brain as two separate entities, but interconnected. The autonomous functions of the brain allow it to conduct repetitive work efficiently instructing the body. The mind directs the brain to perform a few things unrelated to the body brain combine.”

"Okay," Arun nodded slowly, absorbing the explanation. "So, when does Creative Learning start?"

Grandpa's eyes lit up. "Creative Learning blossoms when you stop competing with others.

Competition stifles creativity. Shifting focus to self-improvement sparks inner curiosity and creativity. Rote learning, relying solely on memory, limits deeper understanding and application. Creative Learning ignites a chain reaction—Creative thinking, Confidence, Inclusion, and Leadership."

"But aren't top students in competitive schools creative too?" Arun asked, his voice tinged with uncertainty. "My parents went to prestigious universities."

Grandpa chuckled warmly. "They are, indeed. Creativity isn't absent in competition but shifts from rivalry to personal growth. Competing solely to outshine others drains energy that creative pursuits channel positively. Many achievers—like Steve Jobs, Bill Gates, Mark Zuckerberg—prove creativity thrives outside traditional measures like degrees."

"Thank you, Pops," Arun said thoughtfully. "I understand better now. Do most kids know how to find happiness within?"

"Some do," Grandpa replied gently, his voice carrying empathy. "Others, lacking support, must work harder to unearth their potential when freed to explore. Curiosity and creativity lie dormant, needing nurturing to thrive. Mentors guide them toward happiness and success."

"Go on, Pops," Arun urged eagerly. "Tell me more."

Grandpa smiled, continuing animatedly. "Take music, for example. Everyone feels its rhythm, but not all play, sing, or compose. Like your piano lessons—practice enhances focus and clarity. Information crystallizes into knowledge; intense practice refines it, like focusing light into a laser."

"But why do some excel while others struggle?" Arun queried.

"Persistence in practice matters," Grandpa affirmed. "Yet, each person's limits and mindset influence success. Each possesses a unique talent waiting to be discovered—a journey akin to finding one's 'unique id.'"

"What about people with disabilities?" Arun wondered.

"Even they possess unique abilities," Grandpa assured, pride coloring his words. "Like Einstein, labeled a late bloomer, whose genius reshaped history."

"Piano isn't my unique talent," Arun confessed.

Grandpa grinned knowingly. "Focus and clarity propel success. Coupled with creativity, confidence, and inclusivity, it's a joyful journey to happiness."

"Golden Rule 8, right?" Arun grinned.

"Yes," Grandpa affirmed proudly. "You're perceptive, Arun. Keep exploring."

Arun paused, reflecting. "The rules make more sense now, Pops. They're interconnected."

"They are," Grandpa agreed warmly. "Understanding comes with time. Embrace the process."

"I worked hard on my journal," Arun said, excitement tingling in his voice. "Your guidance pushes me to think deeper."

Grandpa squeezed Arun's hand affectionately, a surge of warmth passing between them. "Phase 2 explores the mind's complexities—your journey now. Unlike Phase 1, where others guided you, this phase is yours to navigate, shape, and learn from."

"Interesting," Arun mused.

"The path isn't smooth," Grandpa cautioned. "Early influences shape self-discovery. Strong foundations ease the journey, fostering gratitude, love, and truth. Weak foundations invite discord, complicating self-discovery."

"Pops, could you give an example?" Arun asked, seeking clarity.

Grandpa: “Imagine a teenager who stays in their room with the door closed and doesn’t communicate well with parents. Parents are afraid of social media’s impact, peer pressure, and drug abuse but have no easy way to say so or restrict the activity. The fear on both sides of upsetting the other is high. Parents can’t let go of their authority and responsibility, and the child can’t overcome the influence of the peer group. The teenager assumes both rights and responsibilities as seen fit. The parents seldom get answers to their questions and the dinner table talk is very much restrained.

If the foundation in Phase 1 is strong, the communication remains open. The mind can easily go through self-discovery and direct the brain appropriately to reduce frictional forces and make the body brain combine work optimally."

Key Points: Application

1. **Transition to Phase 2:** Arun expresses readiness to enter Phase 2 of his learning journey, signaling a new chapter in his life.
2. **Mind vs. Brain:** Grandpa explains the distinction between the mind and the brain, setting the stage for deeper introspection and understanding for Arun.
3. **Creative Learning:** Grandpa emphasizes that Creative Learning flourishes when one shifts focus from competing with others to self-improvement, highlighting the importance of curiosity and creativity.
4. **Creativity and Competition:** Grandpa clarifies that while creativity and

competition can coexist, true creativity often arises from a drive for personal growth rather than a desire to outshine others.

5. **Finding Happiness:** Arun wonders if most children understand how to find happiness within themselves, showing a desire for deeper understanding of emotions and fulfillment.
6. **Unique Talents:** Grandpa explains that everyone has unique talents waiting to be discovered, emphasizing the importance of persistence and self-discovery.
7. **Inclusivity and Confidence:** Grandpa stresses that inclusivity, confidence, and focus are key components of success and happiness, encouraging Arun to embrace these qualities.
8. **The Journey of Self-Discovery:** Grandpa explains that self-discovery is a personal journey influenced by early experiences, highlighting the importance of a strong foundation in Phase 1.
9. **The Role of Mentors:** Grandpa mentions the role of mentors in guiding individuals toward

happiness and success, showing the importance of external support and guidance.

10. **Embracing the Process:** Grandpa encourages Arun to embrace the process of self-discovery and learning, indicating that understanding comes with time and experience.

6.

ANTIDOTE MATRIX

Arun looked up at his grandfather, his eyes filled with a mixture of curiosity and determination. "Pops, I need an explanation on reducing the frictional forces."

Grandpa's eyes softened with affection as he began, "There are several viruses that create frictional forces, Arun. The idea is to eliminate or minimize these viruses incrementally. Let's look at the viruses first. There are many, but I will list ten of them: anxiety, fear, jealousy, anger, hate, guilt, greed, arrogance, attachment, and judgment."

Arun's brow furrowed. "Please give me a few examples."

Grandpa leaned forward; his voice gentle yet firm. "Let's talk about your football game. Would you ever kick a self-goal and make your team lose? Of course not. But viruses like anxiety, fear, and jealousy make you do just that, causing a lot of problems for you.

"Imagine you're afraid of someone at school who might harm you. You hate this person, and anger builds up inside you. You want to attack him but fear his size and strength. Is your anger hurting him? No, it's only hurting you, like kicking a self-goal. What if you spoke to him after talking to your parents or consulting someone, or reported him to the school authorities? It might help. There's no chance if you don't even try. The same goes for jealousy towards a student who gets better grades than you. It doesn't help you; it only makes you anxious and nervous. Competing with yourself instead of comparing yourself to others is the key."

Arun nodded slowly, "Yes, I get it, Pops."

Grandpa's eyes sparkled with pride. "The answers are within you, Arun. Find ways to avoid falling for these viruses for your own good. You'll be pleasantly surprised to know that it's not as difficult as it seems."

Arun's face lit up with hope. "Can I prevent the viruses from entering my mind?"

Grandpa smiled, gesturing towards his phone. "Think about your computer, tablet, or cell phone. Anything connected can get infected. A computer performs better if it's virus-free, just like a human mind. Humans can improve their performance if they minimize these viruses. It's nearly impossible to be completely free of them, as we are always connected to others and our environment. However, greatly minimizing their impact is possible."

Arun leaned in closer, eager to learn. "How do you do that?"

Grandpa's tone became more earnest. "Remember the golden rule 'prevention is better than cure.' When you were a child, you received vaccinations to prevent diseases like polio and tetanus. These vaccines not only protected you but also reduced the spread to others. The same principle applies to computers with antivirus software. For humans, the mind must produce its own antivirus shield. Any outside help is to enable the person to self-produce this antivirus."

Arun's eyes widened with realization. "The mind can create its own antivirus?"

Grandpa nodded, "Yes, the recognition of the three internalized values from Phase 1—gratitude, love, and truth—coupled with Golden Rules 5 through 7, helps the mind produce its own antivirus shield. This logical and practical approach can be put into practice."

Arun's curiosity deepened. "Where does it start? How are humans and computers similar when it comes to viruses?"

Grandpa's gaze was steady. "Both exist in a connected environment, making them susceptible.

The effectiveness of a human's antivirus shield varies based on its strength developed in prior years. No matter how strong the shield is, new viruses are always emerging. Therefore, the shield must continually strengthen. Though challenging, it is well within your capability."

Arun's eyes sparkled with interest. "This is fascinating but a bit complicated. Can you simplify it for me?"

Grandpa's smile was reassuring. "No problem, Arun. We encounter situations daily. Viruses can complicate these situations, but a disciplined mind can build an effective antivirus shield. The process is simpler if the golden rules are well understood and practiced along with Phase 1."

Arun paused his writing, his face reflecting deep thought. "Pops, please explain the details of building this antivirus shield."

Grandpa leaned in, his voice filled with wisdom. "It involves a three-by-three matrix called the 'antidote matrix' to handle the viruses. It's sequential and methodical. About half of it is built by the time you graduate from Phase 1.

"The first step is following Phase 1 (Discovery) and blending it with its natural twin, SOD in Golden Rules. By now, SOD—competing with self, being open to possibilities, and accepting the outcome by detaching from wish—along with discipline (gratitude, love, and truth) should become as autonomous as breathing for those who graduate with distinction in Phase 1. The full spectrum of SOD becomes clearer with age and conscious application to daily situations. It's like a tennis player whose reactions to an incoming ball are automatic, but near perfection comes with practice over many sets, matches, and tournaments."

Arun nodded, absorbing the analogy. "That makes sense."

Grandpa continued, his voice warm and encouraging. "The second step is internalizing an attitude of inclusion, empathy, and humility, which extends step 1. Inclusion diminishes hate and judgment. A confident person relies on inclusion, reducing anxieties and associated negative behaviors. Gratitude and love from Phase 1 and Golden Rule 'compete with self to succeed' make inclusion an easy attitude to adopt.

"Empathy helps you relate to others' problems, making you a good human being. An inclusive mind, love from Phase 1, and Golden Rule 6 (be open to possibilities) foster empathy. Simply saying 'I understand' or 'I feel your pain' can reduce others' agitation and open pathways to solutions.

"Humility reduces ego and encourages interaction on a level playing field, fostering knowledge sharing and input. It's probably the most empowering characteristic, instilling inner calmness and creating room for creativity. Together, inclusion, empathy, and humility shape you into a balanced and respected person."

Arun reflected, "It takes a while to understand."

Grandpa's eyes twinkled with understanding. "I don't mean to simplify a complex process, Arun. Following a logical path with full faith will get you there. The above two steps lead to a place where the seemingly impossible becomes possible. Remember, it is sequential and becomes as autonomous as breath for those who excel in

Phase 1. For the rest, it remains a dream until they regain what was lost."

Arun's voice was filled with determination. "Can I get there, Pops?"

Grandpa filled with unwavering belief. "You can get there with honest effort, not just a wish.

"The third step involves three practices: breath control, being in the now, and being mindful.

"Breath control may sound simple, but many breathe shallowly as they age due to emotions and stress. Fuller breathing balances physical health and soothes mental emotions."

Arun's eyes lit up with determination. "I can practice that."

Grandpa smiled. "Good to hear. Being in the now relieves guilt from past memories and fears of the future, improving focus and clarity. This makes the mind act efficiently with confidence."

Arun's voice was thoughtful. "I have to understand and work hard to get there."

Grandpa nodded. "The third practice, being mindful, helps prevent fleeting thoughts from deviating you from the path. Mindfulness is a winning trait of successful people, ensuring that any deviation from 'being in the now' is corrected on the go. It's called practice because continual practice becomes a habit, making it effortless."

He squeezed Arun's hand gently, his eyes filled with warmth and pride. "The three values, three Golden Rules (SOD), three attitudes, and three practices together form an effective shield to prevent viruses from entering your mind. When they do enter, they are mild. This methodical approach, appropriate to your age and understanding, makes the journey fun and intense. This three-by-three antidote matrix is strong enough to fight known and unknown viruses. When values and right actions become as autonomous as breath, happiness becomes a permanent state rather than an occasional experience."

Key Points: Antidote Matrix

1. Identifying Mental Viruses

- **Common Viruses:** Anxiety, fear, jealousy, anger, hate, guilt, greed, arrogance, attachment, and judgment.
- **Impact of Viruses:** These emotions create frictional forces, causing internal turmoil and self-sabotage.

2. Understanding the Effects

- **Football Analogy:** Kicking a self-goal in a football game as a metaphor for how negative emotions harm oneself rather than others.
- **Fear and Anger:** These emotions do not hurt the object of these feelings but damage the person harboring them.
- **Jealousy:** Competing with self rather than others removes jealousy and fosters personal growth.

3. Minimizing Mental Viruses

- **Self-Awareness:** Recognize and consciously avoid falling into the trap of these negative emotions.
- **Computer Analogy:** Just as computers need antivirus software, the human mind must develop its own defenses against mental viruses.

4. Building the Antivirus Shield

- **Three-by-Three Matrix:** A methodical and sequential approach to developing mental resilience.

5. Phase 1 - Discovery and SOD (Golden Rules)

- **Internalized Values:** Gratitude, love, and truth.

Golden Rules (SOD):

- ✓ Compete with self.
- ✓ Be open to possibilities.
- ✓ Accept the outcome by detaching from wish.

•**Analogy of a Tennis Player:** Automatic reactions become perfected with practice.

6. Phase 2 - Attitudes of Inclusion, Empathy, and Humility

- **Inclusion:** Reduces hate and judgment, fostering confidence and reducing anxiety.
- **Empathy:** Understanding and relating to others' problems, making one a better human being.
- **Humility:** Reduces ego, promotes knowledge sharing, and fosters creativity.

7. Phase 3 - Practical Exercises

- **Breath Control:** Fuller breathing balances physical health and soothes mental emotions.
- **Being in the Now:** Focuses on present actions, relieving guilt and fears, and improving mental clarity.
- **Mindfulness:** Prevents fleeting thoughts, ensuring focus and efficiency of the mind.

8. Implementing the Antidote Matrix

- **Sequential and Methodical:** Each step builds on the previous one, making the process autonomous over time.

- **Internal Strength:** Continuous practice leads to habits that make values and right actions as natural as breathing.

9. Achieving Permanent Happiness

- **Autonomous Actions:** When gratitude, love, truth, inclusion, empathy, humility, breath control, being in the now, and mindfulness become second nature, happiness becomes a permanent state rather than an occasional experience.

7.

Mind and Monkey

Arun looked up at his grandfather, his eyes reflecting a mix of curiosity and determination. “Pops, knowing the golden rules made me understand the antidote matrix better. But why is the mind weak when it has so much intelligence?”

Grandpa's face softened into a thoughtful smile.

"Arun, the mind is like a monkey. It's never still. It's always agitating, leaping from one thought to another. It is emotional, swaying from sadness to happiness, and it can be irrational at times."

Arun raised an eyebrow, a playful smirk tugging at his lips. "So, now you're telling me that I have a monkey in me?"

Grandpa chuckled. "Yes, dear."

Arun's curiosity deepened, his eyes sparkling with intrigue. "I'm curious about this monkey and how to make it behave."

Grandpa leaned forward, his tone both gentle and serious. "It's not a difficult job to start, but it's very challenging to keep it up for long. A monkey is intelligent but lacks a good attention span, making it difficult to harness that intelligence effectively."

Arun leaned in, eager for more. "Please explain."

Grandpa nodded, his voice taking on a storyteller's cadence. "Scientific research found that over six thousand thoughts pass through the human mind every day. Many of these thoughts are repetitive, making a person restless, much like a monkey. These viruses reside in those thoughts. Slowing down this chatter and focusing on what is important can be accomplished through a few minutes of meditation each day. Meditation is a practice in silence. Silencing the mind creates a gap between thoughts. It's not an easy exercise but being aware of your breath is an effective way to slowly silence the mind. I can teach you when you're ready, but remember, you don't get results immediately."

Arun's eyes widened with realization. "Taming the monkey is a must if I want to do well. Once I do that, the mind truly becomes mine. Meditation is for later."

Grandpa raised an eyebrow, his expression questioning. "Are you sure?"

Arun nodded firmly. "How many times I free my mind from the monkey is important. The higher the score, the better the mind. Is there a scorecard, Pops?"

Grandpa smiled, "Arun, it's you and your mind. You want to take the monkey out of your daily life. Meditation and the monkey don't get along well. Eventually, the monkey gives in."

Arun’s face lit up with determination. “Then I need a checklist to know that I drove away the monkey.”

Grandpa’s smile was warm and reassuring. “For now, you need the antidote matrix with you all the time. It’s not difficult once you start practicing it. Like the famous saying goes, ‘practice makes perfect.’”

Arun nodded eagerly. “Yes, Pops. Without practice, I can’t get on the basketball court. Why should this be any different? You keep saying that meditation helps. Could you teach me?”

Grandpa's eyes twinkled with pride. “Yes, later today I’ll introduce you to the preliminary steps of meditation. You can start with a few minutes a day. I’m sure it will help you. You can continue if you are convinced that it is helping you. If not, you can wait it out.”

Key Points: Mind and Monkey

1.Arun's Inquiry:

- Arun asks why the mind is weak despite its intelligence.

2.Grandpa's Explanation:

- The mind is compared to a restless monkey.
- The mind is always active, emotional, and sometimes irrational.

3.Arun's Curiosity:

- Arun humorously accepts the idea of having a monkey within him.
- He expresses interest in learning how to control this monkey.

4.Challenges of Control:

- The monkey’s mind is intelligent but lacks focus.
- Grandpa explains that taming the monkey (mind) is initially easy but hard to maintain.

5.Scientific Insight:

- Research shows over six thousand thoughts pass through the human mind daily.
- Many thoughts are repetitive and cause restlessness.

6.Meditation as a Solution:

- Meditation helps slow down the mind’s chatter and creates gaps between thoughts.
- It requires practice and awareness of breath to silence the mind gradually.

7.Arun's Determination:

- Arun acknowledges the importance of taming the monkey to excel.
- He is eager to know if there is a way to measure his progress.

8.Grandpa's Guidance:

- Grandpa emphasizes that it's about Arun and his mind, not a scorecard.
- Regular practice of the antidote matrix and meditation will help tame the monkey mind.

9.Commitment to Practice:

- Arun relates the necessity of practice to his basketball training.
- He expresses interest in learning meditation from his grandfather.

Varun and Anita

Arun’s face reflected deep thought as he asked, “Pops, it would help if you could give me a couple of examples of how children and their parents handle Phases 1 and 2 and the necessary adjustments along the way.”

Grandpa leaned back; his eyes distant for a moment as he pondered. After a few seconds, he spoke again. “Yes, I can give you two examples that I have come across. These two are about twenty years older than you. One lived in our neighbourhood, and the other is an experience narrated by a friend.

“It’s interesting that you asked me not only about children but also how their parents handle them.

The stories of Varun and Anita that I am about to tell are very different, but equally instructive. Let me start with Varun's story."

Arun's eyes sparkled with anticipation. "Thanks, Pops."

8.

The Story of Varun

Grandpa's voice softened as he began. “Varun was taken to an orphanage by his parents at the age of six. His family had made charitable donations to the orphanage for years and often visited. For his seventh birthday, Varun wanted to spend a few hours with the children there. His mother made sweets, his father bought presents, and all three of them went to visit the orphanage. That visit marked the beginning of a lifelong connection for Varun."

Arun listened intently, his heart warming at the thought of young Varun's selflessness.

"Varun understood the true meaning of love sprouting from his heart as he interacted with children in the orphanage. What he may not have noticed was the empathy building in his mind, the essential attitude from Phase 2 of life. Likewise, gratitude took him to a new dimension as he understood how blessed he was to be born to his parents, who had great temperaments and resources.

"Varun's liking for service grew every year with his frequent visits to the orphanage, and a recognition of his skills pointed him toward neurosurgery. He graduated from medical school and finished a long neurosurgery specialty. One day he wants to be a professor in neurosurgery.

"The important point to recognize with Varun is that his parents were always very understanding and respectful of his needs and thoughts. Love and care are more important to them than material things. Caring parents respect the child's needs, and in this case, Varun is so sweet and highly respectful of his parents, and together they have become a model family. It is important to recognize that there was no instruction book. It was just natural for them, as all three longed to know and support each other and society. They were prepared at every turn to make the most of what was presented to them. This is a clear example of unambiguous practical choices meeting the will to accomplish goals.

"Frequent visits to the orphanage continue to be part of Varun's routine. He seems to have found his Purpose in life. His parents continue to be his mentors, and at important turns in his life so far, his choices have been greeted by chance. He has never gotten carried away with success because he graduated from Phase 1 and Phase 2 with distinction. Varun has covered most of his journey into Phase 3 as he has recognized his Purpose in life and well on his way fulfilling it."

"Varun's story is an exception, not the norm. It

highlights the process of realization of Purpose in life when preparedness meets opportunity. This is the intersection where informed choice aligns with chance as though the universe has conspired to make it happen.

"Varun's passion, a fulfilling profession, and the need for his skills in society, a handsome remuneration, as well as service to society combine to form a good part of the realization of a sustainable Purpose in life."

Arun's eyes widened with admiration. "Wow, that's inspiring, Pops."

Key Points: The Story of Varun

1.Early Exposure to Compassion and Empathy:

- Varun's frequent visits to the orphanage from a young age cultivated deep empathy and a sense of service.
- His experiences taught him the value of gratitude, understanding how fortunate he was to have supportive parents.

2.Parental Support and Respect:

- Varun's parents always respected his needs and thoughts, prioritizing love and care over material things.
- This respectful and supportive relationship helped Varun develop a strong, respectful bond with his parents.

3.Natural Development and Mutual Support:

- There was no strict instruction manual; the family naturally supported each other and society.
- This unambiguous, practical approach facilitated Varun's growth and helped him find his Purpose in life.

4.Recognition of Purpose:

- Varun discovered his passion for neurosurgery and pursued it with dedication.
- His parents continued to be his mentors, guiding him through important decisions and supporting his journey.

Model Family Dynamics:

- The story highlights the importance of mutual respect, understanding, and practical support in a family.
- Varun's family serves as an example of how a loving and supportive environment can help children find their Purpose and succeed.

Arun's reflections and gratitude towards his parents underscore the importance of having a supportive and understanding family, as it facilitates exponential growth with focus, clarity, confidence, inclusion, and Purpose.

9.

The Story of Anita

Grandpa's expression grew more serious. “Anita’s story is quite different. She was full of enthusiasm and energy, always seeking excitement. Her parents were successful professionals but didn’t nurture her creative ambitions. Though they loved her, their love often came as must-do instructions.

Anita reluctantly followed their directions with a heavy heart, her creativity and curiosity unchallenged."

Arun's face fell, feeling a pang of empathy. "That's sad, Pops."

Grandpa sighed. "Yes, it is. Despite no issues with discipline or grades in elementary school, by middle school, Anita's mind began to think independently, and communication with her parents dwindled. In high school, she faced disciplinary problems, including fights and occasional smoking. Her confused parents resorted to blame because they had provided everything, they thought she needed materially."

Arun shook his head. "That's heartbreaking."

Grandpa's voice softened. "Indeed. Parental resources got Anita into a decent college, but she sailed through with bare-minimum grades. She grew close to her roommate and spent a long weekend at her roommate's parents' home. The roommate's mother, a high school teacher, sensed something was wrong and quickly became a mentor for Anita. Empathy replaced authority, allowing Anita to open and see the bright side of her parents' ambitions. Slowly, her anger dissolved, and enthusiasm revived."

Arun smiled, relieved. "That's good to hear."

Grandpa nodded. "Yes, it was a turning point. Anita's new mentor encouraged her to embrace gratitude, love, and truth. Inclusion, empathy, and humility began to find their place in her life. Though not optimal, it made a significant difference. She realized her passion for mass communication and, with her mentor's support, found a good job in the field. Despite this, her relationship with her parents remained strained, and her grades were never satisfactory to her 'tiger mom.' Her dad was always too busy for more than pleasantries and gifts."

Arun looked thoughtful. "I understand why you said graduation with distinction in Phase 1 is important."

Grandpa's eyes twinkled. "Yes, Arun. Anita found Purpose in life, though it remains somewhat hazy. She discovered her strengths, such as being a good listener and synthesizing knowledge.

Overcoming obstacles was challenging due to her weak foundation in Phase 1. Despite finding a good job and mending her relationship with her parents, achieving the three practices of breath control, being in the now, and mindfulness was difficult."

Arun's face reflected gratitude. "Thank you, Pops, for sharing these stories. I'm blessed to have parents like Varun's."

Grandpa smiled warmly. "Yes, Arun, you are blessed with loving, caring, and wise parents. This early foundation facilitates exponential growth with focus, clarity, confidence, inclusion, and purpose. You're blossoming into a delightful young person."

Arun's heart swelled with appreciation as he absorbed his grandfather's wisdom, feeling more determined than ever to embrace the lessons and guidance he had been given.

The Story of Anita

1.Unmet Creative Needs:

- Despite being loved, Anita's parents didn't nurture her creative ambitions, leading to a lack of challenge and dissatisfaction.
- This gap created a sense of reluctance and frustration in Anita.

2.Communication Breakdown:

- As Anita grew older, communication with her parents diminished, leading to disciplinary issues and a lack of direction.
- Her parents' material provision didn't compensate for the emotional and creative support she needed.

3.External Mentorship and Empathy:

- A turning point came when Anita found a mentor in her roommate's mother, who replaced authority with empathy.
- This mentor encouraged Anita to see the positive aspects of her parents' ambitions and helped her revive her enthusiasm.

4.Gradual Improvement:

- Anita's newfound support helped her embrace gratitude, love, and truth, significantly improving her outlook.
- Though her relationship with her parents remained strained, she began to find her passion and purpose in mass communication.

5.Challenges due to Weak Foundation:

- Anita's weak foundation in Phase 1 made it challenging to achieve optimal levels of personal growth.
- Despite finding a good job and mending her relationship with her parents, fully realizing her potential remained difficult.

Key Points and Lessons Learned

1.Importance of Early Foundations:

- A strong foundation in Phase 1 (early life) is crucial for smooth transitions and success in later phases.
- Emotional support, respect, and practical guidance from parents play a critical role in a child's development.

2.Empathy and Support:

- Empathy from both parents and external mentors can significantly influence a child's ability to find and pursue their passions.
- Supportive relationships are key to overcoming obstacles and achieving personal growth.

3.Balancing Material and Emotional Needs:

- Providing material resources is not enough; emotional and creative support is equally important.
- Parents need to balance their ambitions for their children with the children's own aspirations and needs.

4.Mentorship and Guidance:

- Finding mentors outside the immediate family can provide valuable support and perspective.
- Encouraging open communication and understanding can help children navigate their challenges and find their Purpose.

5.Gratitude, Love, and Truth:

- Embracing gratitude, love, and truth can transform a person's outlook and help them overcome past difficulties.
- These values, along with inclusion, empathy, and humility, are essential for personal growth and finding Purpose in life.

6.Examples of Real-life Application:

- Arun requests examples of how children and parents handle the process.
- Grandpa agrees to share stories of Varun and Anita to illustrate different approaches and adjustments.

10.

Integration

Arun sat cross-legged and looked up at his grandfather with a mix of satisfaction and lingering curiosity. "Pops, I've spent a lot of time finishing my journal and feel good about it. But I must ask you a couple of questions to complete my understanding of what you taught."

Grandpa leaned back. "Fire away, Arun. I will keep my answers short."

Arun hesitated, gathering his thoughts. "You haven't said a thing about ego, a word I hear frequently. Isn't it a virus?"

Grandpa's face softened into a thoughtful expression. "Ego not being listed as a virus looks like a gaping hole because it is recognized as the gorilla of all viruses. The ego is an aggregator of several viruses, making it a thousand-pound gorilla showing off its superiority, power, wealth, control over others, and so on. The other side of ego is a timid snake slithering away, fearful of failure, ashamed, and anxious about retaining power and wealth. Ego can be chipped away one piece at a time by the ten components of the antidote matrix."

Arun nodded, absorbing the metaphor. "That makes sense. But you haven't said anything about bullying, which is a big deal in schools."

Grandpa sighed, his eyes reflecting the weight of many stories untold. "A few more viruses I didn't mention before are bullying, superiority and inferiority complexes, and insecurity. I did talk about bullying in our discussion earlier from the perspective of the victim. Graduation from Phase 1 prevents the person from becoming a bully. The courage to fight a bully comes from love of self or concern for others, which you also acquire in Phase 1."

Arun's brows furrowed as he pondered the next question. "You haven't mentioned forgiveness and tolerance as part of the antidote matrix. These are two often-used words. Why then didn't they make the list?"

Grandpa's smile was gentle, reassuring. "Great question. First, the 'be in the now' antidote covers forgiveness. Forgiveness is about what happened in the distant or recent past. Unless one has forgiven, it would be nearly impossible to be in the now.

"The second part of your question is about the absence of 'tolerance,' a highly impactful antidote. However, the attitude of 'inclusion' covers the presence of tolerance. Inclusion is not possible unless preceded by tolerance. This additional explanation of viruses and antidotes is needed to be ready to realize purpose in life which is Phase 3."

Our conversation on Day 1 started with a simple question from you on why people are sometimes mean to others. We have discussed in simple sentences the gist of life and how to make it effortlessly joyful for the rest of your life. There is a lot more explanation needed for educators, intellectuals, and believers in taking a deep dive. I strongly believe that you have got all that you need to be a self-generated spark of happiness and success for yourself and be in harmony with society and nature."

Arun's heart swelled with gratitude. "Thank you, Pops. I feel more ready than ever to face the world and stay true to myself."

Grandpa's eyes sparkled with pride. "You're welcome, Arun. Remember, life's journey is not about perfection but about continuous growth and understanding. Keep your heart open, and your mind will follow."

Arun hugged his grandfather, feeling a deep sense of connection and purpose. As he walked away, journal in hand, he knew he carried with him not just the lessons of his grandfather's wisdom, but the love and support that would guide him through every phase of life.

Key Points: Integration

1.Ego as a Virus:

- Ego is described as the aggregator of many negative traits and emotions, making it a formidable challenge.
- It has two sides: a dominant, boastful aspect and a timid, fearful aspect.
- The antidote to ego involves the nine components of the antidote matrix, which help chip away at it.

2.Bullying and Related Viruses:

- Bullying, superiority and inferiority complexes, and insecurity are additional "viruses."

- Graduation from Phase 1 of life helps prevent becoming a bully and provides the courage to stand up to bullies, driven by self-love and concern for others.

3.Forgiveness and Tolerance:

- Forgiveness is embedded in the 'be in the now' antidote, as it is crucial to move past old grievances to live in the present.
- Tolerance is encompassed by the attitude of 'inclusion,' as true inclusion requires tolerance.

4.Lifelong Journey:

- The conversation began with a simple question about why people are mean, evolving into a comprehensive guide for joyful living.
- Continuous growth and understanding are emphasized over perfection.

5.Self-Generated Happiness:

- Arun is encouraged to be a self-generated source of happiness and success.
- Being in harmony with society and nature is highlighted as a key goal.

6.Emotional Connection:

- Arun feels gratitude and a deeper sense of readiness to face life.
- The bond between Arun and his grandfather is strengthened, underscoring the importance of love and support in navigating life's phases.

11.

Road to Happiness and Success

Arun sat on the porch, his journal beside him, his eyes reflecting a mixture of gratitude and determination. “Pops, I can’t thank you enough for simplifying everything for me. It will be complete if you could relate Happiness and Success to Leadership with a few pointers to practice.”

Grandpa leaned back, a serene smile on his face. "Fair enough. Leadership is an extension of what we discussed. We have gone through the DAP process. You seem to be happy with the discussion and the clear demarcation between phases. Clarity and focus are the two essential mental exercises that arise from the three attitudes and three practices in building the antivirus shield. A successful journey removes or minimizes most of the viruses and transforms the Mind into a Creative Mind, which paves the way to identify Purpose in Life."

Arun's eyes sparkled with curiosity. "Is it a long process?"

Grandpa's smile widened. "Not necessarily. I promise you, the minute you accept that you are in the ring to fight, the rest becomes easy because it is within your power to be a winner. Some may think it is a field of dreams. But it is dreams come true."

Arun's heart swelled with hope. "Pops, that's reassuring. Will you be on my side to help me win?"

Grandpa's expression turned serious yet compassionate. "I don't mean to disappoint you. I can suggest the means, but you are in the ring, and it is your fight. Victory is yours if you believe in yourself."

Arun's resolve hardened. "Okay. The fight, outcome, and consequences are mine. I have what it takes to win."

Grandpa's eyes shone with pride. "Yes. As the Mind transforms into a Creative Mind, Knowledge frees itself from the Mind to become Wisdom, which is the hallmark of a Creative Mind."

Arun nodded slowly, absorbing the wisdom. "It is much clearer now than before, thanks to your added explanation."

Grandpa's gaze was gentle yet intense. "Arun, you are getting into the depths with a summation of the discussion. The Why, How, and What is a summary exploring the secret of happiness and success.

- **Why:** The value proposition that relates curiosity and creativity in a child leading to happiness and success in a methodical way.
- **How:** The autonomous path from the golden rules to the antidote matrix.
- **What:** The hierarchical platform from brain to mind to creative mind to leadership."

Arun felt the weight of understanding settle in his mind. "Pops, there is a lot that goes into getting a full grasp of the subject."

Grandpa nodded. "Yes, there is more. The brain is like a computer and has memory and logic. Mind, the next level up, has knowledge but is nuanced by viruses (distractions). The mind needs cleansing to be effective, and it happens when focus and clarity are brought to bear on the mind as discussed earlier. The antidote matrix plays an essential role in advancing the mind to a creative mind. During this process, the viruses are mostly removed, and the Knowledge in the mind transforms into Wisdom in the Creative Mind."

Arun's eyes widened with realization. "Wow, something to remember. The golden rules clearly say that curiosity and creativity are inborn qualities of a child."

Grandpa's smile was filled with wisdom. "Yes, Arun. These qualities are the foundation upon which happiness and success are built. By nurturing them, you foster a Creative Mind, ready to lead with clarity, focus, and wisdom. Remember, the road to happiness and success is a continuous journey of growth and understanding."

Arun hugged his grandfather, feeling a deep sense of connection and purpose. As he walked away, journal in hand, he knew he carried with him not just the lessons of his grandfather's wisdom, but the love and support that would guide him through every phase of life.

Key Points: Road to Happiness and Success

1.Arun's Gratitude and Determination:

- Arun expresses gratitude for his grandfather's guidance and seeks further clarity on relating Happiness and Success to Leadership.

2.Leadership as an Extension:

- Grandpa explains that Leadership extends from their discussions, involving the DAP (Discipline, Attitude, Practice) process.

3.Clarity and Focus:

- Essential mental exercises derived from three attitudes and three practices help build an antivirus shield.
- A successful journey minimizes viruses and transforms the Mind into a Creative Mind, paving the way to identify Purpose in Life.

4.Acceptance and Effort:

- Grandpa reassures Arun that the process becomes easier once he accepts the challenge, emphasizing self-belief and effort.

5.Individual Responsibility:

- Grandpa emphasizes that although he can provide guidance, the fight and consequences are Arun's responsibility.

6.Transformation to Wisdom:

- As the Mind transforms into a Creative Mind, Knowledge turns into Wisdom, which is crucial for true leadership.

7.Summation of Discussion:

- Grandpa provides a summary exploring the secret of happiness and success through three components:
  - **Why:** Value proposition relating curiosity and creativity in a child to happiness and success.
  - **How:** Autonomous path from the golden rules to the antidote matrix.
  - **What:** Hierarchical platform from brain to mind to creative mind to leadership.

8.Complexity of the Subject:

- Arun acknowledges the depth of the subject, realizing the extensive effort required for full understanding.

9.Role of the Brain and Mind:

- Grandpa explains the brain as a computer with memory and logic, and the mind as having knowledge nuanced by distractions (viruses).
- Cleansing the mind through focus and clarity is essential to advance it to a creative mind.

10.Antidote Matrix:

- The antidote matrix plays a crucial role in transforming the mind by removing viruses and turning knowledge into wisdom.

11.Inborn Qualities:

- Golden rules emphasize that curiosity and creativity are inborn qualities of a child, fundamental for happiness and success.

12.Continuous Journey:

- Grandpa stresses that the road to happiness and success is a continuous journey of growth and understanding.

13.Emotional Connection:

- Arun feels a deep connection and purpose, carrying forward his grandfather's wisdom and support throughout his life.
- These points encapsulate the essence of the chapter, highlighting the wisdom imparted by the grandfather and the transformative journey of Arun towards happiness, success, and leadership.

12.

Leadership

Arun sat with his journal, his heart full of gratitude and a thirst for deeper understanding. “Pops, you explained the secret of happiness and success, and I understood it to my satisfaction. Happiness can’t be complete unless the student relates it to the whole school and community. Would you please open the missing link between happiness and leadership?”

Grandpa leaned back, his eyes reflecting years of wisdom. "Yes, the mind gets activated in phase 2 (Application), a self-discovery process where creativity is unleashed. Creativity is part of a child's activity early on, but creative learning as a process begins when the mind takes over as a self-driving vehicle. Competing with self is the origin of creative learning.

Creative learning leads to creative thinking, as the mind asserts its independence. The sheer joy resulting from creative learning won't stop there. Creative learning becomes empowering and unstoppable, firing away the next step, creative thinking. Creative thinking becomes transformational when focus and clarity emerge as drivers of the mind. This transformation makes the individual confident, fearless, and stress-free.

Confident people are inclusive since they are not competing with anyone. Inclusive people attract others and naturally become leaders. Such leaders build Creative Harmony in the communities they live in."

Arun's mind raced with questions. "How far will I be from becoming a leader once I attain that

Creative Mind?"

Grandpa's smile was serene. "Arun, the Leadership I am talking about is not the same Leadership as recognized now. It is the other side of the bridge that truly makes you a Leader."

Arun interrupted, eager for answers. "Stop there, Pops. You are talking about the other side of the bridge. I am on this side of the bridge. How do I cross the bridge? Give me a break, pops."

Grandpa chuckled, his eyes twinkling. "Don't worry, it is like opening a light curtain to walk up to the destination."

As Arun pressed on, his curiosity piqued. "What is that curtain separating me? Does 'walking up' mean 'climbing steps?"

Grandpa nodded, a sense of pride in his voice. "Yes, you have already climbed the most, only a few more left."

Arun leaned in, eager to learn the secret. "Can't wait. Please tell me, pops."

Grandpa's voice was calm, yet powerful. "Arun, Leaders with Creative Mind infuse a bond of trust, love, and compassion loaded with excellence. They earn respect rather than demand respect using their position or title. They are on a perpetual journey from empathy to excellence. These leaders are spark plugs to invocate the process raising all boats and continually participate in the journey perpetuating the spirit which manifests in excellence shared by many. The world in the technology era is becoming flatter in management and solving problems in a lasting networked environment."

Arun's mind buzzed with possibilities. "Does it mean that my generation will experience a new style of leadership that is more inclusive than your generation?"

Grandpa's smile was reassuring. "Yes, nothing moves in a straight line or appears suddenly. The new generation leaders coming from a creative mindset neither attract attention like fireflies nor will they extinguish their leadership qualities in a short period. They don't seek power; it is inherent in what they do and hence power comes to them albeit slowly. It is an evolutionary process, and you are right in the middle of it."

Arun felt a surge of excitement. “Good to hear, pops. Hope I will be part of that trend and enjoy the journey.”

Grandpa’s gaze was filled with pride. “I don’t want to make it complicated but would like to make a statement. Your knowledge and comprehension are several-fold better than when I was your age. I would have spared myself from painful experiences and failures if I started with your comprehension. Knowledge is cumulative, and each generation benefits from prior generations' experiences.”

Arun, curious as ever, probed further. “I am curious. Where does Varun fit into this Leadership equation?”

Grandpa paused, considering. “Good question. He fits quite well as a quiet leader. He is already doing it by being a person to look up to and talk to for the children in the orphanage. It won’t stop there because his qualities as an unspoken leader promote empathy to excellence in a harmonious way wherever he goes. That is what he will achieve, in my opinion, as a person and doctor now, and a professor in the future.”

Arun nodded, understanding dawning on him. "Good to know. Please tell me how all this relates to Happiness and Success."

Grandpa's expression turned thoughtful. "Success is a symbol or recognition measured by titles, money, power, achievements by various measures. People work hard to be successful and get that recognition. Happiness, on the other hand, is an emotion, shaped by a positive attitude and perseverance, both inside and out. Happiness needs no validation or recognition and hence a long-lasting state of a relatively stress-free mind. This state of mind emits confidence and inclusiveness which leads to leadership effortlessly.

The beauty of the discussion we went through is an exercise where happiness and success inherently lead to leadership in a holistic way. There is a certain way it should be pursued to make it effortless. We explored that "certain way" for you to experience happiness, success, and contentment in life. The process becomes "autonomous as breath" for the graduates with distinction in Phases 1 and 2. Think what happens if breathing is not autonomous. All should strive to master the “certain way” to make happiness permanent (autonomous), not occasional. Arun, you are fully armed now to pursue and enjoy every bit of it.”

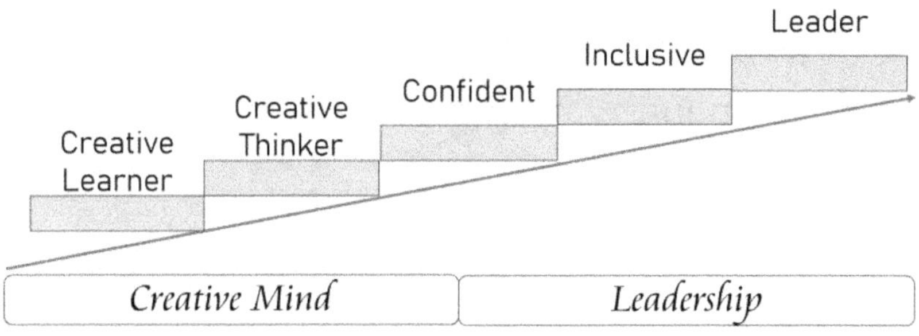

Key Points: Leadership

1. **Creative Learning and Thinking:** Creative learning leads to creative thinking, which is essential for leadership. The process of creative learning begins when the mind takes over as a self-driving vehicle, competing with self, and asserting independence.
2. **Transformational Leadership:** Creative thinking becomes transformational when focus and clarity emerge as drivers of the mind. This transformation makes individuals confident, fearless, and stress-free, qualities that are essential for effective leadership.
3. **Inclusive Leadership:** Confident and inclusive leaders earn respect through trust, love, and compassion. They lead by example, raising the standards of excellence for everyone around them.
4. **Evolution of Leadership:** Leadership styles are evolving, with new-generation leaders coming from a creative mindset. These

leaders do not seek power but earn it through their actions and qualities, making them more inclusive and empathetic.

5. **Leadership Related to Happiness and Success:** Happiness and success are closely related to leadership, as they are shaped by positive attitudes, perseverance, and inclusiveness. Leaders who are happy and successful naturally inspire others and lead effortlessly.
6. **Ethical Leadership:** Enlightened selfishness is essential for progress without harming others or society. It involves aligning personal needs and desires with the greater good, living within ethical boundaries.
7. **Lifelong Learning:** The journey to leadership is a continuous process of growth and understanding, requiring lifelong learning and self-discovery. It is about mastering the "certain way" to make happiness autonomous in life.

13.

The Journey Within

As Arun sat across from his grandfather, he felt a sense of anticipation and readiness. The tables had turned, and now it was his turn to answer the probing questions that would delve into the depths of his understanding and growth.

"Grandpa paused, then smiled. 'Arun, it is my turn

to ask you a few questions, and I want direct answers.'"

Arun nodded, feeling a mix of excitement and nervousness. He was eager to demonstrate how much he had learned and grown through their discussions.

"Grandpa: 'What do you have to give up or sacrifice to be an empowered individual realizing the purpose in life?'"

Arun thought for a moment, reflecting on his journey so far. "I don't think I have a full answer. I don't need to sacrifice anything."

"Grandpa: 'How so? How could you be empowered without giving up something but gain something?'"

Arun's confidence grew as he spoke. "If I don't acquire hate, greed, fear, etc., I have very little to give up. Thanks to my parents and teachers, I don't have a big burden of those. I have a lot to learn by myself and practice. I need focus and clarity. If I unknowingly have harmful viruses, I can give up by maintaining the discipline from the Antidote Matrix. I will gladly give up by exercising my discipline. What is there to worry about when I can get rid of worries?"

With each answer, Arun felt a sense of liberation, as if he was shedding old fears and doubts, making way for a brighter, more empowered self.

"Grandpa: 'Do you remember moral values and practice them?'"

Arun's voice was firm. "What I learned from you is to align my needs and desires with those of society. If they are aligned, why do I have to worry and recheck whether I am a moral person or not?"

"Grandpa: 'Lies and exaggerations are common, and some are harmless. Do you lie if they are harmless?'"

Arun replied thoughtfully. "I prefer not to lie except for jokes. Why should I bother judging whether a lie is harmful or harmless?"

Grandpa couldn't control his amazement listening to the matured answers by his grandson. "Arun, you are at a level I did not imagine. You made my day."

"Arun: 'Thanks, Pops. You have lit a candle in me. I

promise you; it won’t extinguish.'"

Grandpa smiled, a twinkle in his eyes. "On that high note, I can go to sleep happily and wake up to embrace a mighty tall grandson who is on his way to make happiness and success autonomous as breath."

As they sat together, bathed in the warm glow of the lamp, Arun felt a profound sense of gratitude and love for his grandfather. He knew that their bond was not just of blood, but of shared wisdom and understanding, a bond that would guide him on his journey of self-discovery and empowerment.

Key Points: The Journey Within

- Arun's anticipation and readiness to answer his grandfather's questions symbolize his growth and eagerness to share his understanding.

- The questions about empowerment and sacrifice prompt Arun to reflect on his journey and realize that he doesn't need to sacrifice anything if he avoids negative traits like hate, greed, and fear.
- Arun's concept of the "Antidote Matrix" highlights his understanding of maintaining discipline and clarity to avoid harmful influences.
- The discussion on moral values reflects Arun's alignment with societal needs and his understanding of morality.
- Arun's view on lies and exaggerations shows his commitment to honesty and his understanding of harmless lies in certain contexts.
- Arun's gratitude towards his grandfather and his promise to keep the candle of wisdom lit symbolize his commitment to personal growth and empowerment.

14.

SUMMARY

Autonomous as breath for Happiness and Success

Preserving the three inborn qualities of a child—gratitude, love, and truth—and internalizing the SOD approach (competing with Self, Open to all possibilities, and detached from outcome) while adopting an attitude of inclusion, empathy, and humility leads to profound growth.

Just as grass needs rich soil for healthy growth, these qualities need discipline and the right attitude as their foundation. Together, they foster the effortless development of a child into a happy, empowered adult, fulfilling their life's purpose while contributing positively to self, family, society, and nature. Happiness is rooted in creativity, values, confidence, inclusion, and leadership, which should be nurtured from kindergarten to high school to create empowered individuals who contribute to building a harmonious society.

Despite the effortless nature of this growth, humans are constantly exposed to viruses—negative influences—that can disrupt their progress. Practices such as breath control, being in the now, and mindfulness act as a reset button, preventing these negative influences from entering and maintaining the integrity of the body-mind complex.

About The Author

Rao Chalasani came to the US for higher education and later made it his home. After a twenty-five-year stint on Wall Street, Rao decided to devote himself full time to nonprofit causes.

Rao headed the Foundation for Democratic Reforms in India, a US-based 501c(3), from 2000 to 2006. His philanthropic work since then has been in the field of education. He is currently chairman emeritus of the North South Foundation established in Chicago, Illinois.

Rao has published two books in economics followed by a book on human endeavors and excellence. This book, "Autonomous as Breath: Secret of Happiness & Success @ Students & Parents" is a drill down version of empowering young adults to lead a happy and purposeful life.

Golden Rules

1. Curiosity and Creativity are two sides of the same coin.
2. Every child has both for keeps.
3. Everyone has a unique id with unique talent.
4. Prevention is better than cure.

Acronym

S 5. Compete with self to succeed.
O 6. Be open to possibilities.
D 7. Manage choice and detach from chance.

Autonomous as breath

8. Happiness and Success are realizable choices in reach.

Antidote Matrix

Autonomous as breath

Discipline	Attitude	Practice
Gratitude	Inclusion	Breath Control
Love	Empathy	Be in the now
Truth	Humility	Mindfulness

Notes

www.ingramcontent.com/pod-product-compliance
Lightning Source LLC
LaVergne TN
LVHW010928110826
845149LV00013B/2515

* 9 7 8 0 9 9 7 9 8 1 2 5 4 *